The Amazingly GROSS Human Body

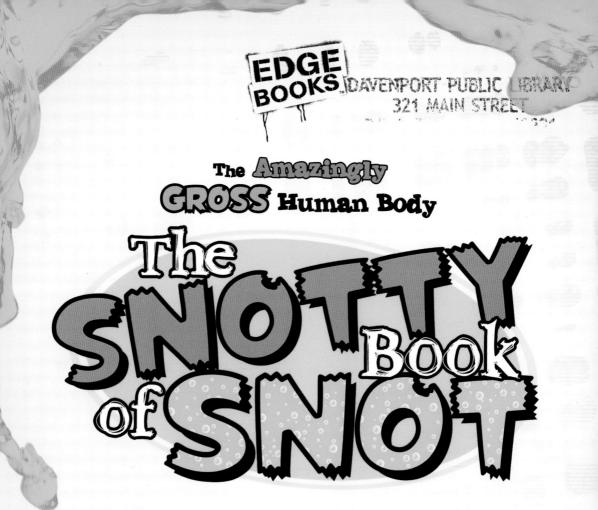

The SNOTTY Book of SNOT

by Connie Colwell Miller

Consultant:
Michael Bentley
Professor of Biology
Minnesota State University, Mankato

Capstone
press®

Mankato, Minnesota

Edge Books are published by Capstone Press,
151 Good Counsel Drive, P.O. Box 669, Mankato, Minnesota 56002.
www.capstonepress.com

Library of Congress Cataloging-in-Publication Data
Miller, Connie Colwell.
    The snotty book of snot / by Connie Colwell Miller.
    p. cm. — (Edge books. The amazingly gross human body)
    Includes bibliographical references and index.
    Summary: "Describes the gross qualities of mucus, and how it works to
benefit a person's health" — Provided by publisher.
    ISBN 978-1-4296-3354-3 (library binding)
    1. Mucus — Juvenile literature. I. Title. II. Series.
QP215.M55 2010
612.2 — dc22   2009005506

Editorial Credits

Aaron Sautter, editor; Kyle Grenz, designer; Jo Miller, media researcher

Photo Credits

Alamy/PHOTOTAKE Inc./Craig Zuckerman, 14
Capstone Press/Karon Dubke, cover (all), 4, 5, 7, 8, 9, 12 (both), 17, 18, 19,
        22, 23, 24–25 (all), 26, 28, 29
Newscom, 11
Photo Researchers, Inc/Eye of Science, 10
Shutterstock/Filipe B. Varela, borders; Sebastian Kaulitzki, 21

TABLE of CONTENTS

SUPER SNOT!

Boogers and loogies. Drips and drops.
Sniffles and snarfs. These are just a few
ways to describe that disgusting fluid
lurking in your nose — snot!

Whatever you call it, snot is pretty
gross. But there's something you might
not know. Snot, or mucus, is actually a
hero in your body's fight for good health.
This icky, gooey stuff works nonstop to
keep you safe from armies of germs.

GROSS FACT

The average person
produces about 1 quart
(.9 liter) of snot each day.

THE TRUTH ABOUT SNOT

Imagine that you're taking a walk to the park. You take a deep breath of fresh air. But that air isn't as fresh as you thought. Suddenly you burst out with a violent cough. Maybe a glob of sticky snot flies out and lands in your hand. Guess what? That disgusting loogie probably just kept you from getting sick.

Dust, smoke, pollen, mold, and harmful **bacteria** fill the air around us. When you breathe, all this stuff gets sucked right up your nose. From there, it's just a short trip to your lungs. Before you know it, you've got more junk in your lungs than your body can handle. Luckily, your snot is there to save the day.

bacteria — tiny, one-celled organisms that are found throughout nature

Snot is always trapping junk in the air
you breathe so you can cough it out.

SECRETS of SNOT

Stiff hairs in your nose help catch dust and germs when you breathe.

Snot is disgusting. How does this nasty stuff keep you healthy? Let's take a closer look.

CAUGHT BY SNOT

When you breathe, junk in the air needs to be stopped before it gets to your lungs. The first line of defense is the wiry hair found in your nose. These hairs catch some of the germs, dust, and other stuff you breathe in. But the hairs can't catch it all. Luckily, a sticky net of snot traps the rest.

GROSS FACT

Many people trim their nose hair when it gets long and shaggy. But to avoid infections, nose hair should never be removed completely.

SNOT FOR DINNER

Microscopic hairs called cilia are found on **mucous membranes** inside your nose. Cilia carry snot toward your throat and away from your lungs. What happens next? You guessed it — you swallow the gooey mess!

mucous membrane	a soft body tissue that makes mucus

Cilia are so tiny that you can't see them without a microscope.

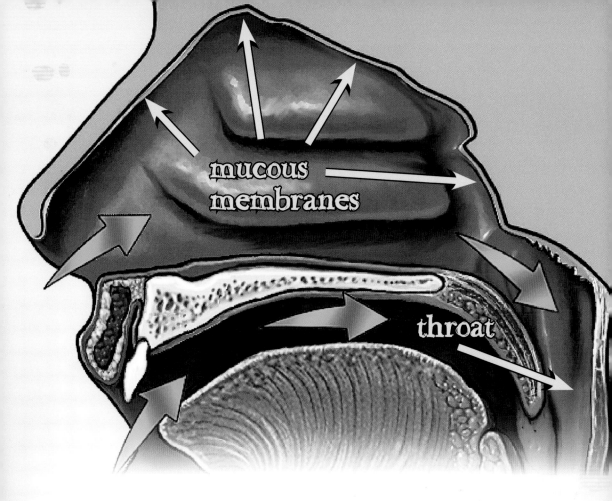

mucous membranes

throat

Without snot, those pesky germs would have gotten into your lungs. But they ended up in your stomach along with last night's dinner instead. Powerful stomach acids then quickly kill the harmful germs. It sounds pretty disgusting. But it's a great system that keeps you healthy.

GROSS FACT

Some sneezes can shoot snot through the air at more than 100 miles (161 kilometers) per hour!

A SLICK GETAWAY

Sometimes, a small amount of snot never gets to your stomach. Instead, it's sneezed out at an amazing speed. Imagine those ugly germs clinging to gobs of snot. They get shot out of your nose and mouth each time you sneeze. That's why it's a good idea to cover your mouth when you sneeze. It's not just good manners. It also helps stop the spread of germs.

You might also cough up a glob of snot known as a loogie. After coughing it up, you can either spit the loogie out or swallow it. If you swallow it, the germs trapped in the loogie are killed in your stomach.

SNOT
EVERYWHERE

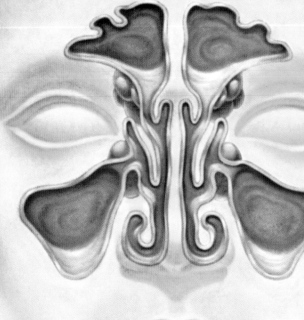

Your sinus cavities are lined with
mucous membranes.

You've probably blown your nose a thousand times. You've sniffled. You've sneezed. You've wiped. You've picked and flicked. Maybe you've even tasted. But have you ever wondered how the sticky stuff is made?

THE SNOT FACTORY

Mucous membranes make snot in your **sinus cavities**. Your membranes make this mix of water, salt, and other chemicals around the clock. Your body can make a big, goobery helping of snot in about 20 minutes.

When you're healthy, you don't even notice your snot. You might sneeze or cough once in a while. But you usually swallow the snot without even knowing it.

sinus cavities — hollow spaces behind your nose where mucus is made

THICK, SICK SNOT

You might wonder — why do you get that annoying runny nose sometimes? And where does that thick mucus come from when you have a bad cold?

Snot really works overtime when you're sick. When germs get in your nose and lungs, your mucous membranes kick into overdrive. They churn out extra snot as fast as they can. They want to flush all those nasty germs out of your body. The membranes also thicken the snot to make it extra sticky. This kind of snot is called **phlegm**. The extra thick snot helps trap more germs than normal.

You probably notice this extra gooeyness when you blow your nose. If the thick snot does its job, you'll eventually blow out or swallow all the germs. And you'll soon be healthy again.

phlegm — extra thick snot made by your body when you are sick

THE SNOT RAINBOW

Most of the time, your snot should be clear. But sometimes it might be yellow. Occasionally your snot might even look green. Why is this?

The color of your snot depends on the germs it carries. When you're healthy, your snot is clear. But if you cough up thick yellow or green phlegm, it probably means you're getting sick.

Snot is usually clear when you're healthy, but it's still gross!

A NOSE FOR WEATHER

Ever wonder why your nose starts dripping when you go outside in cold weather? Your nose is like your own personal heater. When you breathe in cold air, blood vessels in your nose warm the air before it goes to your lungs. The extra blood flow causes your mucous membranes to make more snot.

Moisture from your body also condenses inside your nose. This moisture mixes with the extra snot, and your nose soon starts that pesky dripping.

SNOT'S OTHER TALENTS

Your nose isn't the only place where snot is found. In fact, mucous membranes continually make slimy snot all over your body.

Mucus in your stomach protects you from the powerful acids that break up your food. Without a lining of mucus, your stomach would eat itself up along with your lunch.

Mucus also lines your **intestines** to help food move through your body. Think of mucus as a stream of water that shoots you down a waterslide. The snot is the water, and you're the food. You come out the other end pretty quickly.

Mucus is also found in your ears and in your lungs. Just like the snot in your nose, this mucus keeps germs from getting into your body.

You even have mucus in your urinary tract. These small tubes carry pee from your kidneys to your bladder, and then out of your body. The mucus helps protect your organs from the pee.

intestine a long, hollow tube below the stomach; you have a large and a small intestine.

Mucus Locations in Your Body

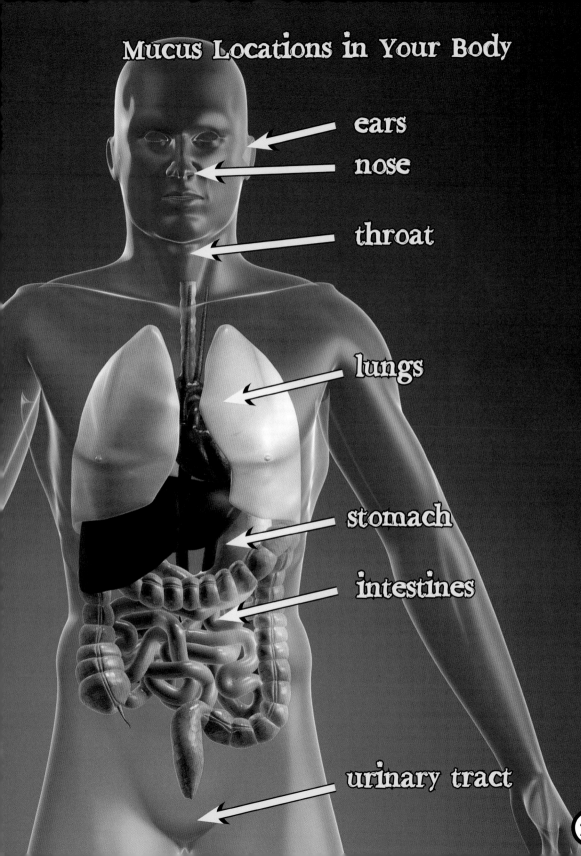

ears

nose

throat

lungs

stomach

intestines

urinary tract

Every nose in the world makes snot.
Why is something so normal also so gross?
There can be only one answer — boogers.

BOOGERS

Sure, snot is pretty gross. But boogers
are even worse. These dried-up, crusty
nuggets of snot hang out of our noses,
waiting to get picked or blown out. That
wouldn't be so bad. But boogers are often
attached to long strings of sickening snot
too. Few things are grosser than pulling
long, sticky boogers out of your nose.

GROSS FACT

According to one study, 70
out of 100 people admitted to
picking their noses. Of those
70, three people said they ate
their boogers too!

THAT'S DISGUSTING!

Most people think boogers are gross because of the manners we learn as kids. But most kids pick their noses anyway. Some even try to eat their boogers.

Mom and dad scold us for this behavior because it makes other people gag. In time, we learn it's something people simply shouldn't do — at least in public.

GROSS FACT

Picking your nose was acceptable behavior in the 1500s. There was even a proper way to do it in public.

Covering your mouth and nose when you sneeze can help stop the spread of germs.

THE DIRTY TRUTH

There's a reason your parents tell you not to eat your boogers. Along with being just plain gross, snot is pretty dirty too. Remember, snot catches the bacteria and other junk you breathe in. That means your boogers are loaded with tiny germs, dust, mold, and other nasty stuff. Putting those boogers in your mouth probably isn't a great idea.

You should also watch out for sneezes. They might seem harmless, but they are packed with germs. It's best to cover your mouth with a tissue when you sneeze. But if you do sneeze into your hands, be sure to wash them afterward. Otherwise, you could easily spread the germs to someone else.

YOUR GROSS, SNOTTY FRIEND

So there you have it. Snot can be disgusting. But it's useful in many ways. It flushes germs out of your nose. It keeps junk out of your lungs. And it keeps your stomach from eating itself up. Snot really is one of your best — but grossest — friends.

ASTHMA AND ALLERGIES

People with allergies often have runny noses. Their noses run because their mucous membranes think things nearby are germs. If you're allergic to pet hair, your mucous membranes make extra snot when you're near an animal. The membranes are trying to flush the pet hair out of your nose.

Asthma is a problem for many people. This condition makes it difficult to breathe normally. When someone with asthma breathes something they're allergic to, their airways tighten and become clogged with snot. People with asthma need medicine to help open up their airways.

GLOSSARY

bacteria (bak-TEER-ee-uh) — one-celled, microscopic living things that exist all around you and inside you; many bacteria are useful, but some cause disease.

cilia (SI-lee-uh) — microscopic hairs inside the nose and throat that push mucus away from the lungs

intestine (in-TESS-tin) — one of the long, hollow tubes below the stomach; the intestines digest food and absorb water and nutrients.

microscopic (mye-kruh-SKOP-ik) — too small to be seen without a microscope

mucous membrane (MYOO-kuhss MEM-brayn) — a soft tissue in the body that creates mucus

mucus (MYOO-kuhss) — a sticky or slimy fluid that coats and protects the inside of the nose, throat, lungs, and other parts of the body

phlegm (FLEM) — the thick snot that is produced when someone has a cold

sinus cavities (SYE-nuhss KAV-uh-teez) — hollow spaces in the bones around the nose where mucus is made

READ MORE

Alton, Steve. *Blood and Goo and Boogers Too! A Heart-Pounding Pop-up Guide to the Circulatory and Respiratory Systems.* New York: Dial Books, 2008.

Larsen, C. S. *Crust and Spray: Gross Stuff in Your Eyes, Ears, Nose, and Throat.* Gross Body Science. Minneapolis: Millbrook Press, 2010.

Stewart, Melissa. *Up Your Nose! The Secrets of Schnozes and Snouts.* The Gross and Goofy Body. New York: Marshall Cavendish, 2009.

INTERNET SITES

FactHound offers a safe, fun way to find Internet sites related to this book. All of the sites on FactHound have been researched by our staff.

Here's all you do:

Visit *www.facthound.com*

FactHound will fetch the best sites for you!

INDEX